ignite

Jabbering with Bing Bong (Anvil Press)

Chapbooks by Kevin Spenst

Ward Notes (the serif of nottingham, 2016)

Pocket Museum (collaboratively written with
Raoul Fernandes, self-published, 2015)

Heavy Metal Mustard on a T-Shirt Bun (collaboratively
doodled with Owen Plummer, self-published, 2015)

Finnegans Wake Versus Pro Wrestling Harper (collaboratively
doodled with Owen Plummer, self-published, 2015)

Surrey Sonnets (Jackpine Press, 2014)

Snap (Pooka Press, 2013)

Pray Goodbye (Alfred Gustav Press, 2013)

Retractable (the serif of nottingham, 2013)

What the Frag Meant (100 tetes press, 2013)

Happy Hollow and the Surrey Suite (self-published, 2012)

ignite

Kevin Spenst

Anvil Press | 2016

Anvil Press Publishers Inc.
P.O. Box 3008, Main Post Office
Vancouver, B.C. V6B 3X5 Canada
www.anvilpress.com

Library and Archives Canada Cataloguing in Publication

  Spenst, Kevin, 1971-, author
      Ignite / Kevin Spenst.

  Poems.
  ISBN 978-1-77214-053-8 (paperback)

      I. Title.

  PS8637.P478I35 2016   C811'.6   C2016-901183-6

Printed and bound in Canada
Cover illustration by Jason McLean
Interior by HeimatHouse
Author photo by Tawny Blythe Darbyshire
Represented in Canada by the Publishers Group Canada
Distributed by Raincoast Books

The publisher gratefully acknowledges the financial assistance of the Canada Coun-
cil for the Arts, the Canada Book Fund, and the Province of British Columbia
through the B.C. Arts Council and the Book Publishing Tax Credit.

to Wendy, Sylvia and Bev

CONTENTS

DATE OF ADMISSION

MY FATHER, THE PHYSICIST

FOR THE NONCE

and it's not his clearing and it's not yours yet this is
where you have come to claim your ghosts
      — Patrick Friesen, *the breath you take from the lord*

What can come from a bed?

a leaf of sleep
a dream cut in half by wakefulness
belief followed by disbelief
you
you again
      — Oana Avasilichioae, *feria: a poempark*

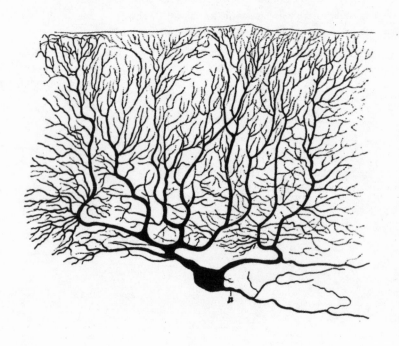

CELL OF PURKINJE FROM THE CEREBELLUM.

WARD NOTES

38,564 etc.
:G. NO___47,800___

NAME		DATE OF ADMISSION
Abraham Spenst	- 2 -	December 12th, 1958.

1958

1959
Jan. 12th.

Jan. 21st.

Feb. 26th.

This patient has been given ... THERAPY December 15th, 1958

Returned Feb. 1.
Jan. 25.

RESULT: Much Improved

FOR ABE

Ghosts on Meds

still cleaving
unreal from the real,
demons from doctors,

prescriptions from
the thrum of foreign hands
so *get off your meds*.

Suspicious of stairs as
they seem up but might
trundle down to basements.

You hover among millions
but I know you, your husky
eyes, ponderous sighs,

your delusions of being
a father. Your Sally Ann
jacket that spirited my

face into an unwashed
hug, a muffled wardrobe
of wept apologies.

Even as your pallbearer,
I ignored your implications,
your chemical-heavy heart,

but only if I see you in some flesh
can I hold a goodbye, say
I'm sorry like it means something.

Ward Notes: Provincial Mental Health Services (1954)

His delusions are religious in nature, expansive and rather grandiose.

In January
the sun is an open-
faced floodlight

mounted above
the horizon. The clouds
are diffusion frames.

The Hollywood
Sanitorium offers
treatment

for a manic episode.
Your supporting
role in an Errol Flynn

feature. Him,
hiding out in rehab.
You, being strapped

down for your big
scene. Your breakaway
moment to swash-

buckle salvation with
Captain Blood and Jesus
playing himself.

The sun sets
the magic hour all day
they can roll

through take after
take. 5 E.C.T.s but they
still don't get

what they need.

Gusts of Sublimation

I have a wild rat in my secrets from you.
— Kenneth Koch

At the summer
picnic the heat slows
everyone's pace.

My schizophrenic
aunt tells me how as a boy
you crawled under

the small house
to root out
a nest of rats.

Her eyes fixed
on my face. She
nods and nods.

I know it was north
Winnipeg, East Kildonan:
Mennonites, and Jews.

Plattdeutsch at home
English outside, your other
mother tongue; the Bible:

stories of authority insulating
the house. But I don't know what
she's nodding about, can't

read her shake of arthritis.
"That's when we knew
something wasn't right."

I don't know what
she's sees in my face.
What could be dead below.

I could hold ignorance aloft
as my new religion. A vestment
of small furs. I too could
have a story no one understands.

Ward Notes: Provincial Mental Health Services (1955)

. . . his work as an ambulance attendant which he found extremely nerve-wracking.

You light up
down Granville Street,
your pride of place

racing away old-world
practices of quiet
Low-German prayers,

an old country rushed off
on a gurney. Then,
another kind of crash.

The doctor listens to admissions
of drinking at shows
in the Commodore, but

nothing *sinful*. You are
in the world, not *of* it.
Your family is your faith;

a belief in church.
Your fingernails pick
at themselves. The doctor

jots down:
no gross abnormalities
were discovered

Guests of Hallucinations

Trees wave over your
arrival in Kitimat, *people of
the snow*. Your first

job away from home,
a rigger on the rugged coast.
You wear the corkboots

of a hard man, hold
a cigarette aloft as snow-capped
mountains glare.

You hear cries in
the fall of cedars scratching
green out of the sky.

You get a blue and red
tattoo of "Mother" on your arm.
A stability badge. You cut

notches around anchor
stumps, swing an ax into a tree
screaming verdant. On

the river hundreds of slippery
slivers crosshatch the light into
a finger pointing at you.

So much foreignness,
you wonder where new
ends and you begin.

Ward Notes: Provincial Mental Health Services (1959)

On this date he was very hostile and could be considered dangerous

Brothers, Sisters and their spouses
hold hands in prayer through a song.

"Praise Father, Son, and Holy Ghost. Amen."

One of your brothers stares at you over
the picnic table of *wareneki, zwieback, platz.*

Between mouths of food the issue of *you*
comes up, your doctors, your medication,

your responsibilities as a new father,
your moral failings, your lack of prayer.

An argument unhinges your face, but
you're fighting on loose ground, sinking

into emotions that stifle movement.
A mother, father, and wife witness

your judgment day, buried up to your
neck in a body that won't reply. Now,

there's no difference between your

arms and the trees of this park, your
torso and the centre of the earth, your tears

and that lake. You dredge everything behind
you for weeks until the day you fill up your

tank, thank the gas station attendant,
leave without paying and get arrested.

It confounds your swirling heart that
they've been sent by your brother. Anger

bellows to give him a piece of your mind,
a quarry of everything behind your eyes.

Geists in Translation

My father begins to see
himself as Jacob on that ladder to heaven.

Jacob's journey up and
between God and the world.

My father has painted
once or twice with his younger

brothers. He climbs
the ladder to start a coat of brown.

The world seems to be
a sign of brightness. A straggly

backyard a manger.
One Sunday my father repents his sins.

Three Sundays later stops taking
his medication, trusts in the Lord with all his red heart.

Abe

God's given me gifts. When I speak it must be in the tongues of
angels. The devil can't grasp these words. My wife won't under-
stand when I follow my lips as the spirit moves but angels will
provide. My daughter babbles in the chimes of angels. She un-
derstands. In this library I'm guided towards the gifts of history.
That librarian is an angel. She takes me to books that explain the
Great Scramble for the heart of Africa and the Great Dig into the
grey matter of our heads. Both races in the 1870s. One plus eight
plus seven is a gift of sixteen. Today is August the 16th. Another
language of angels. I can't write this down or they will know
that I know. Look up casually from this book. Remember how
explorers in the Congo and anatomists in Europe conspired. The
explorers digging for silver, the anatomists dropping silver into
brain tissue to steal routes. To colonize the mind and the map.
Camillo Golgi dropped silver chromate onto a neuron. The axon
and dendrite turned black against a yellow background and their
paths were then stolen for the first time. From there he took the
Golgi apparatus. On behalf of European powers. Africa was pil-
laged by Stanley who took a city, Stanleyville, and next to that
the Stanley Falls. The angels explain how these men stole on be-
half of Italy, England and Belgium, but really it was for a secret
society, a group of half-men from the beginning. *Genesis 6:4*
*There were giants in the earth in those days; and also after that, when
the sons of God came in unto the daughters of men, and they bore chil-
dren to them, the same became mighty men which were of old, men of
renown.* These half-angels grew in greed wanting the smallest
parts of the brain and the largest portions of Africa where they
also took — and this is something the angels have told only me
— the black magic of Bagba and when the brain was opened
later by Wilder Graves Penfield, he whispered voodoo into its
cracks, its sulci grooves. Penfield's assistants thought he was

leaning to look closer, but behind his surgical mask he was whispering words from Africa to invoke the devil inside the brain cells. When the straps were wrapped around my wrists to hold me down from convulsions, they also whispered these words. The devil takes us in shocks of pain, which makes us sin. God has sent angels that move me to counter in whispered tongues. The apocalypse will come in whispers. We will need to escape to a place where there are no European nor African languages. When I step outside the library speak quietly. When the rain falls, we're most vulnerable. It's cold and hard to hold onto this line of thought.

Games of Annunciation

July 5, 1960, discharged in full from this Hospital. DIAGNOSIS: Schizophrenic Reaction Acute Undifferentiated Type. RESULT: Improved

The reds and the red, white and blues
are the colors of the Cold War, but your

decade sighs relief. Three daughters in
matching dresses cut from old curtains.

Their smiles always renewed
in a row of who's lost a tooth

this week. Drawn to the world
with their superpowers of cuteness,

coyness and quickness. They're
a cross between Marvel comics

and the Bronte sisters. Gothic
romances swirling in coloured

panels. A two-bedroom home
with chickens outside, a mother

who works a lot and a father
working off and on, who keeps

them giddy with hugs, bike rides,
clucking jokes and bedtime stories,

who keeps taking his whites, reds and blues.

Ward Notes: Provincial Mental Health Services (1971)

...the patient would not talk to him but wrote him notes saying
he was unable to speak...

I am one of the happiest
days of your life: a boy!

Cigars ceded to everyone
in maternity. A ten-pound

parcel of bliss. Congratulation
calls from family and friends.

I am one of the worst nights
of your life. Crying you awake

when you need sleep for work.
Night after moonstruck night,

as if I were a manic episode manifesto.
Your thoughts wail behind as you race

to the airport to buy a one-way ticket
to China. With no passport your ticket

goes unused. Your doctor's on vacation
and your concern mirrors the concern

on everyone's face, but not again.
You take off your belt, you take

out a letter opener, arming yourself
against the invasion of foreign

chemicals coming down from the mountains
that rise and fall in bawling and howling.

Ghost

I point at the green landscape
from the pop-up book,
fingertip the trees 'til they fall
flattened between hard covers
and your hands in steeple prayer.

Now I lay me down to
I pray the Lord my soul to
If I should die before I
I pray the Lord my soul to

Those are the words you say
to me, those words I remember.

Your weight rocks the bed free.
The glass doorknob turns goodnight.

I fold into a dream of a man
with no name, who answers to no one,

sleepwalking through his conclusion,
the night he transforms our house
into something haunted, panes appealing

to the streets outside, police
come to subdue him — *schizophrenic,*
an agnomen of armies from a strange land.

Thirty-eight, I'm told the story of how
my sisters and I were rushed from our rooms,
driven to stay with our mother's parents.
You, shouting invitations to the heavens:

Everyone is welcome in my house!

a pop-up book, shards of a crystal door-
knob focusing moonbeams to a grasp
of 1977 that opens to an empty bedroom
to a living room couch to a car, shouting
                              up ashes again.

Where the hell was I?

Notes

*. . . he is making his regular visit to his son who is seven years old,
but not at his wife's home . . .*

Listen, there was a time before Facebook,
status updates, before video-cameras

could be pointed at all your family problems
for you to later reflect upon at a film festival.

We were refugees of memory on life-raft
photos that we bound together in albums.

At seven I was already nostalgic for the previous
decade. I took the stack of albums in bright

paisley to the living room floor every night,
studied the pictures: black and whites of my sisters,

a sepia shot of a mangy lion in a cell, an
Aslan without a story. I was on a raft with

a lion who got paler and thinner as the days
wore on through an older form of 3-D

a story to prove that god and fathers don't exist.

Drawing on an Assignment

What does your father do?

My father is a wall
an insurmountable gaze
a cracked floodlight.

What does your father do?

My father is a gate
a subterranean tunnel
a napkin map in a fist.

What does your father do?

My father is an escapee.
My father is the search party.
My father is the judge.

What does your father do?

My father is this blank
drawing paper chewed
spit into mortar.

What does your father do?

My father is the great
escape. Here he is rid-
ing a motorcycle. Here
he is entangled in bar-
bed wire theories of why:
biological, chemical, social.

I can't get over all the things he does.

My Father, The Physicist

"[forgetting] is not something passive, a loss, but an action
directed against the past."
— Michel de Certeau

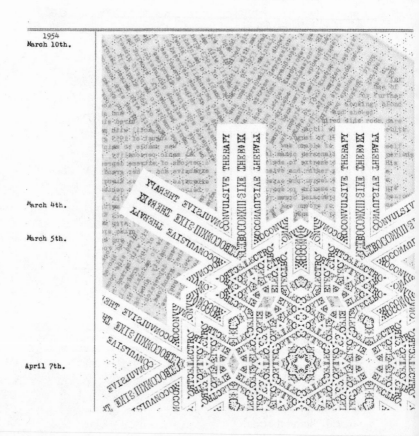

1954
March 10th.

March 4th.

March 5th.

April 7th.

FOR ABE IN HIS COMPLEXITY

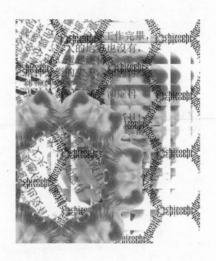

Up

...the increasing tension in the house since the baby was born
has been one of the reasons for his problem although he says
the baby is actually quite good.

—— August 30, 1971

Smiling cooes and piggies
oooooooooooooooooh
through toes, ears, eyes
into an oversized baby.

The receiving blanket
tucked under extra large
cheeks of happily-ever-
afters, a mobile over nights
stored each morning in
a forest of rods and cones,
eardrums taut under the
slamming of bedroom doors.

While high above the father...
  a matryoshka doll of a woodsman sing-songed
                 double to reveal a wolf *innen*
                     half to reveal a sinner sing-singed inside
                         a cell's chemical imbalance, devil-
                            knows-what inside, song-singed

Lullabies incunabula
axed into a cordwood
home with the door wide open.

With first steps taken over
a tangle of legs, routes, immobiles,

it's forest, forest, forest all the way home.

Down

He bashes the red
plastic against
the round opening.
After three straight-
armed attempts, it's in!

His mother claps
His arms mirror
palm against palm,
prototype for an
applause engine.

His father picks him up
spins him until drool
trails like a kite's thread

diamonded by the sun.

Soon his father's head will
bash against the wall of
the psych ward of Riverview.

Certain parts of the brain:
a round dendrite lines up
here, a long axon fits on top,
a neurotransmitter fits in this space,

fits in this space, fits
in this space, fits in
this space, fits in this
space, fits in this space

after a while
a phrase erodes
concave to the touch

a plastic smack against an ear.
The whole body sings a missed connection.

Top

After learning "me" and "I"
but well before my father learns
a restraining order's
between him and our home,
we share some good times.

Remember the back of his bicycle.

I sit on a seat secured over the tire.
Our laughter lolls like exhaust
as we drive over bumps in the lawn,
dandelions losing their heads
between the tires and spokes.

Remember his Suzuki.

The Z holds pre-literate powers in its
70s font blazing like Evel Knievel
sideburns. Gear shift jerk. The smush
of my ear against black foam lining.
The outer shell of my white helmet
presses into his large back. Another
gear shift knock. Fraser Highway's
convenience store shacks blur by.

Until one intersection flips
onto its side and freezes as if caught
in our single headlight.

"Are you okay?"

My open mouth is the reply.

As a child I didn't know what drove him.

A complicated accident to report;

so many words spinning out of reach.

Bottom

After Sunday morning
church, it's t.v. altared
on the living room floor
then the call to borscht.

The bowl beneath my
mouth, a Hieronymus
Bosch of vegetable
damnations (which I
don't understand because
I've gone to church, I've
          said my prayers).

My father lugs his arms
hands over his plate
as if he's manteling to-
gether a machine whose
instructions he's lost at
the back of the garage. Fingers
insert into prayer, his forehead
rests on his elbows creation.
From "Dear God," he goes un-
scripted, pleading for help in
the challenges ahead. I think
he's talking about the borscht.

I put the spoon to my lips
taste a mouthful, a throatful.
Regurgitate gags to bring
          its second coming.

My father's chair shrills
four voices back. He drags
me into the bedroom where
he slips off his belt . . . sighs
strikes my backside straight.

From a yanked-arm angle
the kitchen reappears. My nostrils
over cabbage, tomatoes, onions,
salted in tears, bitter as leather.
I hate him and soon he'll be gone,

sighing over an Arborite table
behind Cathedral-sized windows
of glass triangles. When I'm

taken to see him at Riverview
Hospital, it's worse than borscht,
worse than the belt. An eyeful of
                         unfamiliars.

Visits continue like Sundays,
which I don't understand
because I've said my prayers
in murmurs that dint my knuckles.

Abram

Surrey, August 11, 1977

Lord, remind me it's my brain behind my difficulties. Remind
me in minutes and in days. The Bible as my path to follow. Jesus
as my Lord, Savior and Hero. In the beginning your spirit
hovered over the face of the depths. This verse teaches us how
our faces are over the depths behind our own eyes. Our bodies as
a reflection of your creation. The brain, the core of a little earth,
with eyes as oceans, our face the mountains and outside every-
one orbits. Help me hold to this truth from the Bible so my
thoughts don't spiral smaller. Keep my thoughts at home. For-
give me Lord for wandering too deep into the science behind
this sickness. I'm suffering a chemical imbalance, but I must also
hold onto my faith in you. When I saw how dendrites were like
trees, like the cross itself, I believed mind was the only landscape,
but it became a demented Golgotha empty of your glory. A for-
est of darkness and caves. The world exists but it comes into the
eyes upside down and the brain corrects it, but mine doesn't. It
turns the world sideways. It spins the world into puzzles which I
mistake for my hands. We'll keep groping around and around
into smaller and smaller games. Smaller than atomic particles,
quarks called up, down, top, bottom, charm, strange. Dangerous
and empty. Keeping us away from your word. You are the way,
the truth and the life, but I feel a fall into something else. Each
thought is a ledge that crumbles until my head is a pathless cliff.
Lead me not into stumbling temptation. I need to walk with
you. What a day that will be when the spirit sets me free in
heaven where there are many rooms. In that eternity where
there will be no confusion. My father has many rooms, Jesus
said. Everyone is welcome in my house. We can all be saved. I
can be saved from this if I believe in you. I must trust you and
not my medication. Up, Down, Top, Bottom, Charm, Strange,
the angels that sing inside everything. There are times when it's

the chemical imbalance, but other times when it's my weakness
to see how a room is a single place where we can all gather to
sing with the angels *how great thou art.*

Charm

Insofar as it is possible, Mr. Spenst has been assimilated into the ward society and has participated in activity therapies. He is not a very social individual...

—June 1, 1978

1.

Fingers march along the tops of hymnals towards the tip of a two-inch pencil, a weapon to draw warfare on donation envelopes. My mom's closed purse at my feet, the offering plate hovers overhead like a UFO. Words from the preacher, alien instructions, my mom's prayers press into her palms.

2.

"Your father's sick," my mom explains, winding past dogwood, willow and hemlock. We park in front of a large brick building. We step into a large room. Men are scattered like botched replicas of Rodin's thinker. My action figureless father cornered in a wheelchair.

Two men play checkers at a table, casualties of the unknown, trenches buried in their brains. My hands in my pockets.

3.

When we meet on the outside, it's at Guildford Mall and I hurry to the toy store, to the wall of Star Wars characters. His wallet offers up a ten-dollar bill. We sit on a bench and he talks while I tear Luke Skywalker from his movie backdrop packaging. Walk him along my lap as shoppers pass swinging plastic bags of what they'll soon become. At home I play on shag carpet. Luke Skywalker steps into a hooped thread. He pulls and pulls and tries to tear it free.

46

4.

"My mom lets me use matches," I lie to my cousins one sum-
mer. We soldier toys into the garage. The spit of a spark and a
flame masks the face of an erstwhile Han Solo whose mouth
drops to a rosy glow. Laughter idles from my throat into the
empty garage. My cousins think I'm crazy: "Those are going to
be worth something someday!" Once boredom settles in we
walk to the park. I toss the faceless figures into a ditch. The
quondam Obi-Wan plops next to an empty stubbie with the label
soaking off. My hands in my pockets. Reliquaries emptied of he-
roes.

Dark Matter

Mrs. Ward wipes the "d" from her name as a warning of things to come for Dennis.

Heads down, thumbs up, 7-Up! calm darkness in the crookhollow of my arm and desktop.

Mrs. Ward is old but she has comic books we get to draw from if we finish early.

Dennis is adopted or something, has problems. One day she dumps out the contents of his desk.

We play a version of tag on the monkey bars where we have to touch each others crotches.

When I ask to borrow a ruler, Dennis puts his hands in his desk like he's playing piano.

In detention Dennis pulls down his pants, mooning Mrs. Ward whose back is turned.

My desk is crammed with notebooks, textbooks, *MAD* and *Crazy* magazines. My ruler is covered in layer upon layer of white-out and doodles. The tip of my pen sinks softness.

One day my dad shows up at the window. I'm taken to talk with him at the hopscotch court.

Each time my head goes down I'm gathering shame; I don't know what my classmates know.

I draw superheroes on my ruler in small panels: exemplars of strength, confidence, abnormality.

Mrs. Ward points Dennis to the door, her arm flab flaps. The class clown to the office.

I chase Dennis down 160th. I swing a stick at him; he backs up and up all the way home.

No surprise visits in Junior High School. I'm taken to visit his transformations at a psych ward, then a halfway house, then the hospital, then his rooming house, then the hospital again.

I don't know if I'm on the side of good or evil. I hope to some-day wear wide funny ties.

Strange (1984)

My sister's driveway arrival rumbles. I glide up steep steps from
the basement to see her Mustang. At the kitchen table Mom's
gaze drops back to the calculations of bills.

Comb my hair, muscle on layers: mac, jean jacket, headphones.
Metal quarrying rock from my Sony walkman until eardrums
are shrapnelled dull.

Out the front door to my sister's honks for me to hurry up or
our home to get out of the way. She slammed the front door
goodbye at a young age. Housing now handled elsewhere. She
pops Joan Jett into the stereo and *I love rock and roll* growls and
the sugary Go-Gos on the other side of the tape. A secret for this
drive. Too loud to talk about anything or anyone.

We roar up the Fraser Highway, pass a couple behind a clattering
cart of bottles, past a stretch of forest between brand-new con-
venience stores, past an auto-wrecking yard and onto the curve
of a narrow bridge to New

Westminster to Dad's bachelor apartment. We creak up wooden
steps to a glass front door. My sister buzzes. He's out before her
finger lifts. Hugs her, hugs me, leads us into his room: bed, bar-
fridge, table with an open Bible, a pack of apocryphal cigarettes.
"Lunch at the Sha-Sha Club is always a good deal," he says, look-
ing for eye contact, hoping old confessions from the asylum
won't leak between his lips or eyes:

*I am a police officer on duty — an ambulance driver. Did you see people
dying in Korea? I can bring them back to life . . . I have been separated
three and a half years. It hurts too much.*

I go into his bathroom, study his portrait in prescription drugs: thioridazine, chlorpromazine, trifluoperazine doubled in the mirror, chemicals like stars that season his moods, extended equinoxes.

When he stops taking his meds, calendars crash from the sky. I know it'll soon happen again. In the mirror you see the future: a landscape you have no control over. Lip synch Quiet Riot's *We're All Crazy Now.* Don't leave the bathroom.

Quark

In a basement suite in Delta he reaches
for instant coffee on an otherwise empty shelf,
the aneurysm announces its presence,

How great thou art, plays from his Radio Shack stereo.

The fall of his body into a destructible
table announces trouble to his landlord
who hurries down, calls an ambulance
while standing on coffee powder.

Then sings my soul.

I answer the phone by the kitchen table,
my sister's voice collapses under the news.

At the hospital, our family encircles
a bed, life-support about to announce his ascension.
The window brings light into the room.

But it's wrong, the doctor's wrong, tears are wrong.

Eight years in an Intensive Care Unit wrong,
his grandchildren growing up like shoots in a makeshift
playground around a compost heap body.

Thy power through the universe displayed.

Eight years his daughters fold his frailty to fit him
into his wheelchair. His body slouching loose.
Sometimes they feed him lunch or dinner
until he slowly herds his features from the spoon.

He survives with a large print Bible (NIV)
as life-support, faith held in rickety paths
between axons, dendrites, glial cells.

If there's a heaven I hope
he's there. If there's a god, I
hope he's dead so that everyone
can spin each particle of time
                          as they see wholly fit.

For the Nonce

I call to ask about property taxes
and you tell me about the light...
the way it comes in through the window

— Rhea Tregebov

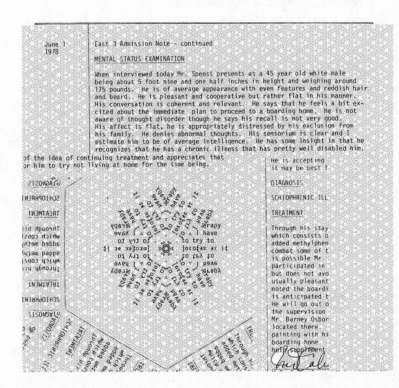

"MARGARET"

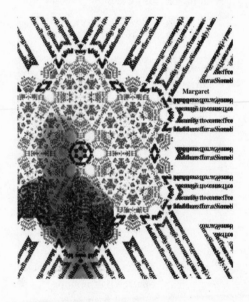

Dendrites of Passage

Recover Dad's hospital haircut crown,
worn from strung-out thoughts pulled
through the top of his head, stranded
nervous tissue that roped his moods royally.

Touch a second into a hold, a body
whirled again. Dad gave airplane rides
that cost an arm and a leg, a ligature of
laughter over grass, a stump into stars

synapsed into headfuls of touchwood—

Glue huffed in that zip-lock mask: base-
ment dizziness glazed shame over a father
shivering outside the five or six rings
upstairs. But I didn't want to pick it up,

schizohaptic—
                 schizoocular—
                                schizo—

Hardly stayed still long enough
                 for me to spell him down.

Then, a turn to an intensive care room: Dad
fallen from a stroke, left half undone.
His face overthrown, his body hollowing
beneath a blanket moss green. To hold his last
hand, broken twigs ending circles of certainty.

His eyes combust blue heat, his head
burns into spikes. Who could dust
fingerprints from these voluted flames?

Smallest of Theories

Thinking is schizophrenic. Thinking abstracts us to bricks. Thinking tricks us into thinking it is doing more than thinking. Thinking thickens a wall of ratiocination that separates the Cogito from the Children of the Senses. Thinking fortresses us with a sense of strength and certainty. The walls are dressed in jackets or T-shirts — whatever suits the times. Within thinking theorizes straightjacket talks. Thinking has no eyes or ears or advice. In its syllogism of movement, thinking is a brick-limbed behemoth that flattens the world with every step. Thinking — with or without a book in its mouth — is cave-man talk. Thinking convinces us that animals don't think. Therefore, *thinking apes*. Thinking is brick by brick. In a home where there is no wholeness of hugs, understanding of eye contact, wisdom of *how are you?* thinking cogitates its edifice. Thinking builds a labyrinth of walls. Thinking thinks through the escape route in thought. Thinking is every abstraction you could ever imagine bigger and bigger. Thinking is masturbation. Therefore, not without pleasure. Thinking is pants around ankles and Ginsberg's howler held out for all to see and a hand going back and forth over the deconstruction of liminal linearity and circumscribed circumcision. Therefore, inappropriate. Thinking thinks the same no matter how different the articulations. Thinking is a wonder: that it should masturbate from a straightjacket! Thinking thinks thinking smallest is impossible.

(In the Middle of the B&E)

— for three sisters

Midway to White Rock for supper at our mom's,
we rubberneck the demolition of where we grew up.
The yard's half bulldozed into a heap of busted heirlooms,

an acre of landscape scrapped behind a dollop
of nostalgia along the frame of our used-to-be house:
glassless windows, graffiti from some schlup.

My sister pulls over, we walk back into dirt-hemmed clothes.
A house B&Eed three times until mom bought an alarm system;
now it stands stripped, exhibit A to a burglar's old boast.

I once climbed all trees and walls of that shady kingdom
surveyed traffic into the distance of down-the-road,
fell asleep in the basement bedroom to the traffic's hum.

I ask my sister to boost me back into a childhood mode,
reach and muscle myself up and through the bathroom
window into gloaming. I move like moonlight slowed.

Walls are now ghosts and 2x4s panel a dusty gloom.
I x-ray vision through two bedrooms, a suspension
of disbelief, superpowers to save someone from Dr. Doom.

I walk between posts into memory's concoction of a kitchen,
no 8x10 of our family (together) smiling blondly on the wall
or the dishwasher where I wished away plates and cognition.

At the stairs to the forever unfinished basement I stand still,
remembering the knife left by the thief on my bed, missed
because I'd gone to church. Agnostically I descend the steps' fall.

When I reach the cold cement I am taken to this
room which was my sister's and then became mine
after she left the ins and outs of the door-slamming business.

Under her bed a collection of hubcaps like signs
of the getaway she planned with her boyfriend,
the one who'd taught me to scrub clean the guts of engines.

Next to brick I feel a light switch cover and it bends
under my fingers, breaks into a potsherd of darkness for home,
a five-finger discount on a relic from where the story ends.

for supper we have pasta al dente and conversation that roams
into crime and the budding of Surrey grow-ops, what our old house
might have been its last ten years. My mom shrugs, passes the yams,

proclaims success at helping others with computers, as if she were Moses
leading her retired neighbours into the promised land of technology,
all the world from the comfortable chair she sits in when her door closes.

Her world, *where neither moth nor rust corrupts, and where thieves
do not break in and steal.* She sows virtual farmlands, seeds of happiness,
never purloined by beloved or stranger, slipped in a mystery up her sleeve.

Cellular Sonnet for the Nonce Sonnet in Prose

I'll never forget the time when that sperm
broke into the egg and I was made me.

Halcyon seconds egging on production   meiotic exertions done on the double
I was a little gamete game for anything   doubling nodes sounding off meiotically.

Made the most of cramped quarters   a new quartet of faces that came and went
maintained roots in spite of divisions   gametocytes breaking off into new camps

"ergo, ego, I go gig," aleatory translations   but never nodding from physical labours
and I decided I should keep track of things   that warm interphase in my diary
                                                                        of seconds.

Those were the days all parts hustled and bustled and then nine months later I was born to grow up to earn a living listening to international students' first memories from the age of three to six of a father handing a toy to his three-year-old son in the hospital in Germany and just the blue of that shapeless toy remembered forever, (*gibs* means cast in German and cast in Japanese where they think it's an English word) of a Japanese boy learning to read from *hiragana* written on his hands, a *ne* that looked like the smile of a cat, a *neko*, (Yasu was the Japanese student's name but in Korean his name means beast) of a Korean boy's tale of being taken at the age of six by his grandfather to one end of Seoul and left to return by subway on his own, (*opa* in Korean means older brother but in German it's grandfather which in Arabic is *Jed*) a Saudi's first beauty contest for camels and the fear of being under such lanky heights crying until he was comforted home, (where the English word cozy sounds like a Saudi rice dish with twelve spices), all stories to establish a similarity of starts, a past-tense lesson in an ESL classroom pulling up irregular verbs, reaching down into the cool dark to feel for the shapes of certain roots.

Flutter-Stuck Flights

for Lara

Three crows perch around the rim of a basketball net.
If I stopped to teach them to fly through or just shut up,
I'd be of some use to our world so full of noisome complaints,
but I continue to walk along the path through Pandora Park.

If I stopped to teach them to fly through or just shut up,
my obsessions would leave me be and I'd relax in your company,
but I continue to walk along the path through this park.
I have an appointment with a therapist whose head angles like a bird.

My obsessions will leave me be and I'll enjoy your company,
for not all insights are reached on the mountain peaks behind me.
I have an appointment with a therapist whose head angles like a bird.
Epiphanies penciled in before lunch in a softly furnished office.

Not all insights are reached from the mountain peaks behind me.
Decisions made from within soon flutter their way without
epiphanies penciled in after lunch in a softly furnished office.
She draws a "thinking-feeling-acting" triangle that looks like a beak.

Decisions made from within soon flutter their way without
I wonder why I'm paying a hundred dollars for doodles.
She draws a "thinking-feeling-acting" triangle that looks like a beak.
Her ever-present question chirps: does that make any sense?

I wonder why I'm paying a hundred dollars for doodles
but she wins me over within a gaze that watches with care.
Her ever-present question reassures: does this make any sense?
A problem is the world at an unexpected angle slipped into a knot.

She wins me over within a gaze that watches with care.
We must learn to fail towards perfection (if culture's taught us anything).
A problem is the world at an unexpected angle slipped into a knot.
With enough knots collected, they scaffold a fine nest.

We must learn to fail towards perfection (if culture's taught)
to be of some use to our world so full of noisome complaints.
With enough knots collected, they scaffold a fine nest.
Three crows perch around the rim of a basketball net.

Do Not Go Before the Blazing Coronation

I wasn't raised by wolves but by women,
though we've been mistaken for a pack of huskies;
our sharp blue eyes ensnaring eye contact.

My sisters dressed me as a dancer in fine linen;
I laughed through character changes with ease.
I wasn't raised by wolves but by women.

My mom sang, *don't let the wolf eat the children,*
before night shifts as she searched for her keys.
Our sharp blue eyes ensnaring eye contact.

My father was a wrinkle across abstraction,
an attempt to tame the wiles of a problem.
I wasn't raised by wolves but by women.

A grave man, a good man, a wild man's prediction,
my father rages still: a forest crowned in fire;
our sharp blue eyes that sparked eye contact.

He passed before he could pass along a fraction
of that territory between a whisper and a whack
I wasn't raised by wolves but by women
our sharp blue eyes blooming eye contact.

A Song from Bedlam

"For I am not without authority in my jeopardy"
                              — Christopher Smart

Let my father be Christ the Lion
(on special occasions), Freud
once or twice on Jeopardy,

the King of New Westminster,
of cigarettes, of strong-armed tattoos.

Let his phantom mind into
shadows, soap bubbles, TV;

everything a shimmering mirror
to feedback a sleepless loop,

until days of stasis on the couch
suspicions slipping beneath cushions

fears of coins as listening devices.

Let nerves like webs stretch
from his eyes and ears into

the speaking places
peopling the living room.

Let a spider named Alex feed
him answers on his La-Z-Boy

until this poem is weighted with
enough images to take on its own

existence,
muttering to itself

about spinning out spaces
from a flat surface to your eyes.

Problems were game shows
haywired with tangents;
he was one unique contestant.

Daylight Savings

Monday, this Korean's first day.

First,
orientation
around the block
(the Marble Arch's history
of strippers,
the Russian mob not mentioned)
and then
he sits down
with me in a glass-
walled classroom to determine his level

"Please answer in complete sentences with as much detail as possible,"
I say like a handshake.

After each mistake
                    that he makes
                                    he fights a flinch.

He studied in the Philippines since...
                            for three months
                    (*prepositional problems with tenses*)
in order
            to progress his English further.

For each microexpression of discomfort

I imagine a bird flying
                    into the window
                                    behind him.

This man becomes one of fifteen assessments.

If I see them at school,
                I'll smile but they'll have forgotten
                                me in that cascade of first-day faces.

Later in the week on my way home
                traffic on Richards is blocked: there's someone on the fifth

floor of the Marble Arch
                  throwing
                        belongings out his window:
                (*possessive pronoun uncertainties*)

a Wayne Gretzky hockey game,

        hockey

           sticks,
                  record,

      books..

                (*articles?*)

Everything falls or floats
                to the sidewalk,
                      street and cars.

He kicks a glass pane
             out and then the metal
                  frame itself.

The police rush into the building

                                with weapons I've never seen before.

            (limited vocabulary)

Today the window is boarded up. Other windows in the buildings are boarded up. With almost thirty windows it makes a kind of advent calendar. Once every glass window is smashed, the building will be taken down for Christmas and everyone — Koreans, Canadians, the police, Wayne Gretsky fans, Wayne Gretsky himselft, grammarians and birds — will sing a goodbye carol.

On First Looking into Chapman's Face

Cracking up isn't hard to imagine:
anything round with two marks
makes a face that's watching you.
Usually something alien or grotesque.

That railing pulled from the wall
left three holes where there
once were loose screws: thus
eyes and an open mouth lip-
synching recurring thoughts.

This room you return to every
night, an echo of the room you
grew up in. This room on the fifth
floor of a building held up by
shouts, rodents, duct-taped posters.

You collapse on an uncomfortable cot
stare at the doorknob metres away;
it's the cold glare of a stranger
unlocking your epic failings
babbles batrachomyomachia,

a stack of books from the library
seems like an Easter Island head.
A smiling face on a game you've
carted around your whole life.
Hockey sticks as noses. Faces multiply;

necessity bursts from your mouth:

Everyone out. Now!

spilling mistayks in vankuwver

akronyms skrable th skoolscape,
iLac, PGIC, PLI, WCC
as if lisence playts on bildings,
as if thay wur all parkt
iydling, wayting fer th loot
too mayk thyr gedaway

gowld rush aftr gowld rush is BE SEE's
histry, frum lumbre as gowld in trees
to fillm sets stryking it rich

insayde a skool I tot studnts
wile holiwould aktors kist on
a red mowdurcykle in historik gasstown
an entyre day to surkle a kis
wth kamera krews in tayk aftr tayk.
Evry fayv minuts we touk a brayk
so stuwdnts kood watch and showt
adooration frum th windoes

We wur studing TOEIC,
an akroynm fer a test
amungst uthers: TOEFL, IELTS,
test aftre test t tayke
aftre tayke

sow students kun get jawbs
with Monsantoe in meksico
or Krapht in kolumbia or
millton bradley in japon,
or sow stuwdents kun
understande holiwould movies

71

or just feel freedum elsewhere
thruw disguyses in th mowth
knew consononts as kostumes

at nite I reed bill bissett
n feel at howm in wurds
thut downt need to be kleend up
in ledders that petishun fr new sownds.
snooozin into hystorical dreems

FACTS RELATING TO JOHN MORTON

Mr. Arrived in New Westminster
B.C. in the year 1862.
afterwards. preempted from

the government
all the land
Mr. Arrived

west of
Burrard Street to
afterwards. preempted from

Stanley Park.
All.
Mr. Arrived

died very
wealthy
afterwards. preempted from

passing away
on the 18th day.
Mr. Arrived in New Westminster
afterwards. preempted from

JOHN MORTON, VANCOUVER'S EARLY PIONEER

written by his son, Joseph,
a carbon copy of the father
unsuccessfully
published

emotion bequeathed,
inaccessibility.
"all I have" is the "Rooms,"

Joseph Morton not employed,

spends time
experimenting with
his basement.

references his father

a beautiful legend

Joseph Morton died in the Asylum
for the Insane, New Westminster,
on 2 March 1933.
never ceased to talk of designing
his father, and the fraud and man-
ipulation of the obsession.

MEMO OF CONVERSATION, 12 SEPTEMBER 1935

(Whilst photographs sat)

Mrs. Morton: "Joseph was one day old when his mother died;

Mr. Morton and I went down to Westminster; a circus came to me.

(Note: this indicates that after the first Mrs. Morton died, he had to place his little baby son Joseph in the care of his friends.)

We saw the circus camels and elephants, and when he got back, Joseph told us all about the big animal gusto,

about

one of them having a tail at both ends."

Straps of Roots

Weighted with ancestors
as numerous as the stars
after a shock to the head,

my father's first shake
from electroconvulsive
treatment in 1954.

Clinical confidence
swabbed his temples
for a new lineage
        of headlines.

    name tags, name names

Freud was given
a Yiddish one—
Schlomo
after a grandfather.

Jung was born Karl
after a patriarch
who loved poetry
but turned to medicine.

Jung named the fleeting forms
that scratch the corners of corneas:
shadow, anima, animus –
archetypes in his sights.

After handshakes, friendship,
and photographs,
Freud and Jung mud-slung each other
tracked separate paths
through jungles of nomenclature

while their coeval, Paul Eugene Bleuler,

in 1908 bagged the biggest
unknown of all: *dementia
praecox*. Renamed it
schizophrenia,

a declaration of hope
flagging new treatments:
hydrotherapy, discussions
with therapists, an hour a day
planting flowers, pulling
weeds like fistfuls of lightning.

Bleuler grafted Greek
roots that *split* the *mind*,
the lunar pull opening a notion.

name call, name drop

Four years after my father's birth,
Ugo Cerletti and Lucio Bini
plugged psychiatry into the stunned
face of an outlet.

110 volts for half a second

charged through
the psychiatric circuit

How much would go through my father?
Did he read the categories on the dials:
intensity, frequency, pulse width?

Did it convulse him back
to youth when everyone's
head is electric
light bulbed every second?

The line of his name a filament.

    name part, namesake

In my hands
my father's soft-
touched report cards
from 1940 to '45.

In Grade 2 reading C, then
B, B to an A in grade five,
by grade six down to a D.

Would a schizophrenic
biographer look for words
hidden through the years?

        CBBAD
        cabbala bad
        cabbed
        bed

Or was D the mark
of another bogeyman
emerging from the crawlspace
under the small house
growing feral
between his feet
running up his body
to knock his blue eyes
from the words
of his Grade 6 reader?

> caught a decade later,
> in the name of Ugo Cerletti,
> in the name of Lucio Bini,
> in the name of Bleuler,
> in the name of Jung,
> in the name of Freud.

A genealogy still dialed today

in volts that cleanslate
autobiographies.
Sequestered lightning
a conspiracy of stars.

Pastoral Tenses

to imagine a language
   is to imagine a form of life
                        — Wittgenstein

Imagine a verb tense routine
where life is an undisclosed lesson,
this Sunday afternoon I gaze up
at entangled tangents of branches.

I'm imagining slow and steady growth
as I stretch out under mottled
shade and uncut grass gloves my hands.

I imagined these words in your mouth:
grammar is a habit of the mind
that none of us can kick,
a habit that huddles us elsewhere,

or these:

Home reworded me with nothing
with nothing reworded me home.

Home relettered me with little
Moeh, oehm, emoh, hemo

Little me with relettered home.

You'll have imagined me boggled,
but when I looked for your form
            you will not be there.

80

And once again the sun has gone down,
you have been any of the shadows,

confused into tenses and language games.

An alarm will clamour me to the same
present tense, the same dream of time
where it lays out its tidy auxiliaries
along a part of the brain yet to be named.

> *life forms imagine to is*
> *language*
> — not Wittgenstein

Etiology of a Heartbeat

Walking is such easy progress.
Finger on a ring in a pocket,
mind in a circle of a thought.
Narrative underlies here to there

Progress is such an easy illusion.
Cottages reflect into the evening
lamped with crystaline insides.
Dusk, your face softens shadows.

Illusions are so easily solved.
This oar bent by the water
or straightened by the moon.
Repetition into reputation.

Solutions are easy on lips.
I'll row you into the middle
of the lake and stop thinking.
Ask you to marry me quick,

write out all the nonsuch roses,
promise a child down the road
stand in the doubling of families.
Now a dream alters into I do:

our rings clink on metal railings.
Inside, touch patterns a promise,
fingers planing this new gravity.
Hands held tightly as if home.

Glossolalia

Now I know there is no one to blame,
but that impassive god
who shoots stray bullets
through the brain.
> — Margo Button's "Culpa"

try, try, every time try to plow out lungs with try,
try heaving and hoeing dirt from dactylic depths
try to forge tries to nails to hammer our shambling
shanty from two-by-four false-starts, newlywedded
heartwood and stucco phantom limbs that hold try,
try to saw the night we first into a load-bearing beam
try, try to palm ramshackled walls off to a ceiling
with trillions of try, try, tries sticking into our home,
a welcome mat at the front door to declaim
> *Now I know there is no one to blame,*

stoop under the trials and tribulations of try, try,
try, try to withstand the song of weather sturming
und dranging outside try, try, try to elbowroom
a closet into a bedroom, into a babyroom for its thumb
lengthening try, try, try, try, try to babble-talk
back into its index pointing like a lightning rod
to be struck with electric words from us
its mother-father sky and clouds, try, try, try
even as breathing grows odd. Oh,
> *but that impassive god.*

try to shift-work prayers from aorta to ventricle
breathe in heuristics to trick lungs to labour

harder into the sun's slant to *try, try, try, try*
to step into the forest crouched in Jack pines,
into a darkness of moon-made leaves,
to poach from nyctanthous lined rivulets
lure whatever weight I can to *try, try, try* to catch
a flash and hurry back through this stranger's property,
a mash-up trash-talker with a carpet-long mullet
                              who shoots stray bullets

try, try, try to breathe out gestalts to scout
broken branches over trip-wired worries
set to loop a leg up and upside-downsy wits,
a dangling of arms, a dewording of try, try
try, try to bring back a small fish cinched in a grip
try, try, try to sweet-talk it to grow fatter than lean
try to flavour it into a salad of hand-me-down roots
at a table made of our outstretched arms as we talk of things
that can be filled: mirrors, beds and sudden terrain
                              through the brain.

84

Domesticated

Sometimes it's best to take a long run at housework:
today I sprint three blocks up Pandora and jog
back along treeless Triumph whose rooftops and chimneys
recast the North Shore mountains and clouds.
Bounding inside I stab Dirt Devil's tail in the wall;
he roars infernal across rugs and into corners
snorting warrens of dust-bunnies.
He roars over my habit of cursing housework.
Jog to job, it's a multi-step system for smiles;
you'll be home in an hour. Winding these thoughts back
along a vacuum cord I think of how we've given
each other a range of rages and joys, but today
the basics will suffice. In time, when our maybe girl
toddles across floors, she'll fall clean into footsteps wild.

Domesticated Double

Sometimes it's best to give yourself up for adoption.
After weeks considering a dog, we come home
to a cat lazing his matted length across our door.
He looks like a black and white newspaper thrown down
for some other spirit moved in. Don't know where
he's from: summer, a river... his hobo markings
headbutt our hands which lure him inside, but tuna
juice instigates purrs in our home. Each day
he wears a different name: Panda's perfecting
his hobby of yawning. Loci's claws skate mischief
on wood laminate, Pablo Neruda's tail flicks
angles as if code for a cat-thief partner outside.
Shed hairs involve more dances with the vacuum;
when he hears its howl, he scatters in footsteps wild.

Vancouver Special

Poetry is a community project in which we are all participants
— Sachiko Murakami

The neighbours' front yard fonts
guarded by statutory grandiosity.
Will our family make the loan?

Into the mental health equation,
a child with a mortgage mouth?
The neighbours' front yard fonts

To whom is rustic assigned?
What Verdana can anyone afford?
Will our family make the loan?

How to make a signature of home
the good grace of a sprinkler?
The neighbours' front yard fonts.

Tittles glitter like stucco, afford-
ability becomes a character in a fable.
Will our family make the loan?

Flat wood, veneer becomes
a forest of forms to wander into.
The neighbours' front yard fonts.
Will our family make the loan?

Body Made Mantra

Things secret, and Ignote.
— George Daniel Ecclus. xlii. 60 (1639)

Let there be a centre of self
stringing together deictic dynamos
of here and now. Might thumb
and forefinger draw the double
helix down, open the blindness
to see outside the blueschist home.

Let there be a stick along a picket-
fence, a spinal cord chorus
knocking across resolve,
bone concaving to must
marrowed in skeletal properties.

Let attention stencil mandalas
into the medulla, stamp the brain-
stem directions for breaths
to be blessed and heart-beats
to synch with hellos and goodbyes,
stretching legs beyond the block.

May mandalas circle discs down
as imprints of passing strangers,
ideograms of blossomed ideation,
flowers from brick-and-mortar folly,
new constituents of continents afloat.

Until nerves longitude down
to conus medullaris, tail endings

give latitude to frame our new
proprioception from those first
two consonants that flinted
together ignivomously

to heat sweet apartment, canvas,
soup, debate, handshake, inkwell
                    home away Aum.

Abram Bernhard Spenst

Canby, Oregon, December 4, 2011

In the spirit of my father, a feeling comes cloaked in lamb's
wool, comes cloaked as a prayer. It's Sunday morning in
America and the price of my family's stay at my sister's is that
we attend my brother-in-law's new church. Hear him preach at
Bethany Evangelical. A weekend of shopping at outlets
redeemed in the blood of the lamb. The songs are familiar and I
open my throat to sing. I cough. "Unleashed for God," reads a
banner on the wall. Educational programs for troubled youth
and soup kitchens are explained. The deacons with their
ploughshared permits in their wallets allowing them to carry
concealed weapons. Their wives raising their hands to the beat
of the drummer on stage within a glass sound booth. An entire
rock band behind my brother-in-law as he asks us to close our
eyes in prayer, tells us how God accepts us for who we are.
Blotches and all. I don't believe a word of it, but I hear
acceptance in his voice. In the spirit of my father, I let this
resonance that must be beating through everyone (even for my
mom who's snoring next to me) be called God.

Axon "Blueberry" Hillock

My father, Abram Bernhard Spenst, second generation
Canadian of Mennonite stock, soup, and slurps.
Born in Winnipeg, in East Kildonan, to parents
who spoke Plautdietsch, a kombination of German
und Dutch. At the elbow-to-elbow kitchen table, he
chewed through new consonants from kindergarten.

A teen at the top of the '50s, a decade rooted
in aortal sediments, Abe wooed the girls with love-
me-tender lyrics in his convertible beneath the aspens
outside Abbotsford. Under his palookaville cap
he winked love blue-eye to blue-eye into the happily
ever after heart of a good Mennonite girl. (No dancing
at their wedding of *faspa*, gifts and stern advice.)

In the early '60s he started speaking to angels under ashtray halos
who told him his province was an abbreviation –Before Christ.
Abomination whispering all around, he palpated to the airport
to buy a one-way ticket to China to seek asylum for his wife
and three daughters. His spinning eyes tipped the airline desk
to call the credit card holder. My mother refused the purchase,
begged him to come home. The private contacts in his head
babbled him elsewhere: hospitals, mental institutions, boarding
houses, nights sleepless in a car or on a bike through weeks.

Three more decades dervishing, dropping, coming home, dervishing
dropping, coming home — a son being born — dervishing, dropping.

The final eight years of Abe's life slowed to magma, half-
paralyzed in a hospital bed, weekend outings in a wheelchair.
Visitors strained over his stroke-broken schizophrenia,
his tongue rustling over a stubbly underlip, speech mumbled
numb. His false teeth like an old phone by the side of the bed.

Abram Bernhard Spenst, a name spoken into hands cupped
in prayer. A swirl of words decanted into a twister to lift
leaves from a gravestone at a Mennonite cemetery on a hill
of Thiessens, Seimens, and Klassens. Power lines chirp above,
like those summer nights we fall asleep under open windows.

under the tree again

In   a   north-   east   patch of the   park,

beneath   hundreds of branches   of   leaves   large   and

higher   up   small,

I stretch   g r a s s w   a   r   d   s   under   the gloaming

and   the   view   above   of   sky-

blue   eyes   through leafing dusk   sets

darkness   behind.   lids

at   rest.

Good dreams can be forecast   falling asleep through such sights.

NOTES

"Dendrites," "Nodes of Ranvier," "Abacus," "(Dates of Admission)," and "Strange (1984)" won first place in Lush Triumphant Literary Awards: *subterrain magazine* (Vancouver), 2011.

"Down" appeared in *dirtcakes: literature and art in (re)spite of* (Rancho Santa Margarita, CA) Spring, 2013.

"straps of roots" appeared in *Prairie Fire* (Winnipeg) Winter, 2011-12.

"abram," and "quark" first appeared in *CV2* (Winnipeg) Spring, 2012.

"A Song From Bedlam" appeared in *Moonshot* (Brooklyn, NY) issue 4, 2012.

"Abram Bernhard Spenst, Canby, Oregon, December 4, 2011" appeared in *in/words* (Ottawa) Winter, 2012.

"Flutter-Stuck Flights" appeared in *Fifth Wednesday Journal* (Lisle, IL) Fall, 2011.

"spilling mistayks in vankuwver" appeared in *the Maynard* (online) February, 2011.

Axon "Blueberry" Hillock" appeared in *Rhubarb Magazine* (Winnipeg) Summer, 2011.

"Do Not Go Before the Blazing Coronation" was translated into Chinese by Laifong Leung and read in English and Chinese at Sun-Yet Sen Garden for the Chinese-Canadian Translators Association, Summer, 2014.

ACKNOWLEDGEMENTS

Gratitude is extended wholeheartedly to the UBC Creative Writing Program, two years that changed my life. I was introduced to poetry by Keith Maillard, shown its limitlessness by Ray Hsu, and taken into its keen heart by Rhea Tregebov. My cohort taught me about tawdry enjambments and all the other particulars of poetry; thank you Elizabeth Ross, Karen Shlanka, Ben Rawluk, Christine Leclerc, Emily Davidson, Andrea Bennett, Margaret Bollerup, Kim Fu, Michelle Deines, Lauren Forconi, Anna Maxymew, Nathalie Thompson, David Mount, Jordan Abel, Taylor Daniel Ashman Brown Evans, Melissa Sawatsky and Lucie Krajcova.

Thank you Barry Ledwidge for helping me decipher the medical and institutional terminology in the psychological reports on my father. Thank you Rhea Tregebov for helping me gain access to them.

A tremendous thank-you to Daniel Zomperelli for giving me the opportunity to co-edit an issue of *Poetry is Dead*. Nikki Reimer and I chose the topic of mental health and it has made all the difference.

I'm very grateful for the overflowing talents of Jason McLean who made original art for the cover. Cheers, Soupy!

Thanks Shane Neilson for giving this manuscript a push.

I want to thank Anvil Press for being a second family. Brian Kaufman and Karen Green have provided tons of support. *Merci beaucoup!*

Without the unconditional support and love of my mother, sisters, brother-in-laws, and nieces and nephews, I never would have had the confidence to explore the emotional terrain in *Ignite*. You are all the centre of my world.

This is my second book with Anvil Press but it was written before *Jabbering with Bing Bong*. Consider it a prequel. Neurological underpinnings. Time travel. Foundational.

Tawny, will the next book be about you? xoxo

ABOUT THE AUTHOR

Kevin Spenst, a Pushcart Poetry nominee, is the author of a previous volume of poetry, *Jabbering with Bing Bong* (Anvil Press), and ten chapbooks, including *Pray Goodbye* (the Alfred Gustav Press), *Retractable* (the serif of nottingham), and *Surrey Sonnets* (JackPine Press). He has done a one-man show at the Vancouver Fringe Festival and over a hundred poetry readings across the country. His work has won the Lush Triumphant Award for Poetry, been nominated for both the Alfred G. Bailey Prize and the Robert Kroetsch Award for Innovative Poetry, and has appeared in dozens of publications including *Prairie Fire, CV2, BafterC, Lemon Hound, Poetry is Dead*, and the anthology *Best Canadian Poetry 2014*. He lives and works in Vancouver, B.C. where he's an enthusiastic participant in a number of writing communities.